The Art of
PRESSED
Flowers

Sylvia Pepper

RUNNING PRESS
PHILADELPHIA, PENNSYLVANIA

A QUINTET BOOK

Text copyright © 1989, 1990 Quintet Publishing
Limited. All rights reserved under the Pan-American
and International Copyright Convention.

First published in the United States of America
in 1990 by Running Press Book Publishers.

Reprinted 1992

ISBN 0-89471-858-4

This book was designed and produced by
Quintet Publishing Limited, London

Creative Director: Peter Bridgewater
Art Director: Ian Hunt
Designer: Annie Moss
Project Editor: Mike Darton

Typeset in Great Britain by
Central Southern Typesetters, Eastbourne,
Manufactured in Hong Kong by Regent
Publishing Services Limited.
Printed in Hong Kong by Leefung Asco
Printers Limited.

This book may be ordered by mail from the publisher.
Please add $2.50 for postage and handling for each copy.
Running Press Book Publishers
125 South Twenty-second Street
Philadelphia, Pennsylvania 19103

Contents

Introduction

Flower pressing is a rewarding craft. Beginners and even children can achieve pleasing results right from the start, while those interested in developing their skills can go on to produce truly exquisite work.

Not so long ago, most people thought of flower pressing as merely the creation of pictures. But you can make pendants, paperweights, pill-boxes, trinket boxes and many other small and enchanting items. The possibilities of producing something exciting and unusual are great.

Few other hobbies offer so much variety, and the chance to express creativity. The fun of choosing flowers as they grow is as much a part of the process as pressing and arranging them. After all, what could be more delightful than to go outdoors on a warm summer's afternoon and gather a collection of richly colored flowers and foliage? Returning from such an expedition and savoring the tumble of colors in your basket is something to look forward to. Knowing the setting from which they came and seeing them in their freshly-picked glory will inspire you when it is time to create arrangements.

Once picked, the flowers must be put in the press. Then, six weeks later, comes the really interesting stage. It's a joy to see just how much of their original beauty your flowers have retained, and to see which ones still have their true colors. Some will have changed colors and developed a new and different kind of beauty.

The most exciting stage is creating designs. Attractive designs will almost arrange themselves if flowers are picked in the right conditions, pressed correctly, and their color combinations are carefully chosen. Above all, you must be receptive to the many ideas suggested by the flowers themselves.

There is pleasure, too, in creating specially designed gifts with pressed flowers. A beautiful wedding present can be made with tiny wild pansies and 'lucky' heather; a spray of locally picked flowers can cheer a homesick friend far away. A floral birthday card that has been carefully and lovingly made by hand will be treasured for years. Pressed flowers are ideal for other simple gifts, such as bookmarks, tiny pictures or even pendants.

The techniques needed to make such items are simple, but guidance is essential for the novice. This book helps you learn how to collect flowers, and explains the process of pressing — how long it takes, ways to get the best results from

different types of blooms, and handling dried flowers.

A separate section explains the process of drying flowers in their original three-dimensional form, as a prelude to making a selection of attractive and long-lasting winter flower arrangements. The illustrated selection of flowers and foliage suitable for pressing include tips on how to make the best of them.

By pressing and drying flowers, you can preserve beauty — while at the same time creating something new. There is no ends to what you can do, there are so many ways to produce beautiful work. For those who love flowers and enjoy making beautiful things, the time you take finding, selecting and pressing flowers will be repaid in good measure with all the satisfaction this craft has to offer.

Pressing

EQUIPMENT

One of the great advantages of this craft is that you can start without spending very much money. In fact it may well be that you already have most of what you need at home, and that a variety of everyday household objects will now become the essential tools of your craft. It is a good idea to assemble the following items.

The most important piece of equipment is, of course, something in which to press the flowers. This could be simply a large book, or it might be a flower press specifically designed for the job.

An out-of-date telephone directory is ideal as a pressing book because it has the right sort of absorbent paper. Books with glossy pages are unsuitable as they can encourage mildew. A second advantage of a phone book is that it does not matter if its spine is eventually damaged by the thickness of the layers of flowers. (Naturally it would be unwise to use the family bible or any other treasured volume for this purpose!) Whatever large, expendable book is used, additional weight is necessary for successful pressing. This could be provided in the form of other books or bricks.

Although the phone-book method can be perfectly effective, a press is preferable. This is because it puts the flowers under greater pressure and therefore speeds the drying process. Also, carefully prepared flowers are rather less likely to be disturbed by having the separate layers of blotting paper and corrugated paper placed on them from above, than by the sideways action of closing a book.

Many craft shops and quality toy shops now sell flower presses. These are fine – but avoid making the mistake of buying the smallest ones, which measure about 4in (10cm) square. The disadvantage of these is that, although they are pretty and can be used effectively for small flowers, they have severe limitations if you want to press such essential elements as grasses and long, gracefully curving stems. The ideal size for a press is about 9in (23cm) square. Larger ones can become very heavy and, unless they have some special device for maintaining pressure in the middle, the two pieces of wood which sandwich the pressed material may develop a tendency to bow or warp. The result of this is that the flowers in the middle are under less pressure than those around the edge, and are therefore at risk of shrivelling or becoming mildewed.

BELOW AND BELOW RIGHT Useful tools. *1 A fine soft brush to tease off slightly sticky pressed specimens from their blotting paper beds, to move delicate flowers around during design work, or to brush surplus pollen from flowers such as buttercups. 2 Pencils and pens for a variety of jobs, from indexing storage books to doing decorative line work. 3 Cocktail sticks or toothpicks, for applying tiny amounts of glue to flowers. 4 A ruler – metal if possible – to ensure straight edges. 5 A retractable craft knife for cutting card and mountboard, preferably of the type that has a blade with several snap-off sections, so that the blade is always sharp. 6 Scissors: a large pair for cutting paper, fabric and other material and 7 a smaller pair for use with plant material. 8 A small pair tweezers for picking up delicate plant material or for working with various jewelry-type settings.*

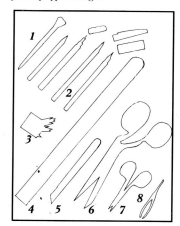

FAR RIGHT TOP A finished press, together with a lightweight travelling press.

FAR RIGHT BOTTOM Some of the many richly colored velvets which make ideal backgrounds for flower designs.

Making Your Own Press

This is relatively simple and should ensure that you get exactly what you want in size, weight, the number of layers, and so on.

MATERIALS FOR MAKING A PRESS 1 Two pieces of sturdy wood such as plywood, measuring about 9in (23cm) square and ½in (1cm) thick (9-ply is ideal and should not warp). 2 Four 3in (8cm) bolts with wingnuts to fit. 3 Three large sheets of blotting paper. 4 Some stiff corrugated card which can be cut from packing material.

Rub down the surfaces and edges of the plywood with sandpaper. Place the two pieces together, one on top of the other, and drill holes large enough to take your bolts in each of the four corners, about ¾in (2cm) from the edge; fix the bolts into the bottom piece of wood, gluing the heads securely into position. Cut 12 8in (20cm) squares of blotting paper, trimming off triangular pieces at the corners to accommodate the bolts; cut 7 pieces of corrugated card of the same size and shape. Starting and ending with card, interleave two pieces of blotting paper with each layer of card. Place this card and blotting paper 'sandwich' on the wooden base; locate the top piece of wood on the bolts and secure the wingnuts.

You might also find a lightweight traveling press an ideal companion on a country expedition. It can be made on the same principle as the sturdy press, but smaller and lighter.

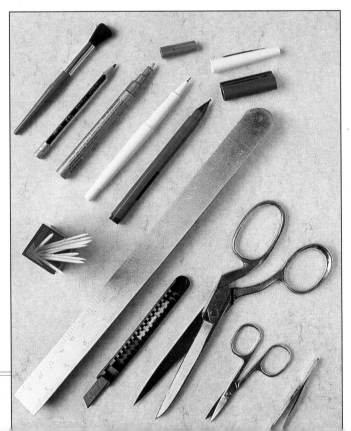

Storage Equipment

You will need to find some means of storing pressed material in good condition until you are ready to use it. This should be easy because, whether or not you have used old telephone directories for pressing, they certainly make excellent means of storage. You may find it useful to keep several of these books, each one reserved for a different type of plant material.

Some people prefer to store each type of flower in an individual bag. This method is fine, if the bags are porous so that the flower can 'breathe'. Plastic bags are not recommended: they could trap any remaining moisture. The ideal bag for the purpose is one which has a paper back for porosity, and a cellophane front for visibility. If bags are to be used, a convenient means must be found of keeping them under some pressure. Inside telephone books perhaps?

Amid the paraphernalia of the flower presser's craft, decorative flowers (including alstroemerias, sweet peas and pansies) await their transformation into decorative design.

Design Materials

When you are ready to begin making designs, you will need a range of materials. Most of these should be as easily available as the equipment described previously. Items required include design backgrounds, such as paper, card or fabric, as well as glues, and some protective coverings.

Paper or card should be of good quality and have an attractive color and texture. In addition to the materials that can be purchased from art and craft shops, the range of ordinary colored writing papers now available offers a delightful choice; moreover, plain areas of thin card are often to be found in suitable colors and sizes on attractive packaging material.

It is preferable to use fabric as a background for most flower designs. This is because its range and subtlety of color and texture is even greater than that now available in paper and card. Patterned and heavily textured fabrics are obviously not suitable for design backgrounds, but almost any fabric that looks good with flowers will do.

ABOVE A typical pressing book, used here for pressing heather. Additional weight is provided in the form of two bricks.

Velvet has a rich depth of color which changes according to the angle at which you look at the design, and becomes lighter in color where greater pressure is applied (around the edge of a picture, for example, where the veneer pins or locking plate grip most firmly). Satins have a beautiful sheen, and are suitable for use with the most delicate flowers.

Acquiring fabrics should not involve too much expense. It is not necessary, for example, to purchase the most costly dress satins: lining satins can be just as attractive and, although velvet is usually expensive, you require only small pieces and might discover just what you need on the remnant counter. Remember also that either furnishing or dress-making fabric will serve the purpose; any plain-colored leftovers from other handiwork can be put to good use. Best of all, you might be fortunate enough to acquire one or two out-of-date swatches of plain fabric color samples, as used in large furnishing fabric departments. You would then have an amazing range of colors from which to choose.

All but the sturdiest fabrics are easier to work with if they are given more body by being backed with a self-adhesive covering (of the sort normally used for such purposes as covering shelves). Any pattern is unimportant, for it will not show.

The most important type of glue required is the one that sticks the flowers to their background. For this purpose, I prefer to use a latex adhesive which can be applied in tiny amounts on the end of a cocktail stick. You may also need other types of glue from time to time, including one for bonding paper and card. This is most conveniently available in the form of a solid adhesive stick.

Once a design has been glued into position . It should be covered in some way that ensures permanent protection for the flowers. A variety of materials may be used for this purpose: clear self-adhesive covering film, varnish, resin, acetate or glass.

BELOW LEFT Two examples of the sort of colorful fabric swatches which you might be lucky enough to acquire from the furnishing fabric departments of large stores.

BELOW Design backgrounds backed with a self-adhesive covering to give them more body. (Apply this backing before cutting the background to size.)

COLLECTING FLOWERS

*I*f you are lucky enough to have somewhere to grow your own flowers, your work may begin long before the collecting stage. There is the delight of choosing the seed packets most likely to produce blooms good for pressing. Then there are the pleasures of planting the seeds, tending the young plants and watching them grow to maturity.

When collecting flowers for pressing, the aim should always be to pick the best specimens in the best conditions. This is relatively easy with flowers picked very near your home since you can choose just when to pick them. Several factors should be taken into account when deciding on the optimum time for picking.

Flowers must be picked at the right stage in their development. This stage is usually reached shortly after they have emerged from the bud, when their color is at its richest. Occasionally, buds are more useful to the flower-presser than the open form, as in the case of tightly closed dark-orange montbretia buds. Many designs are enhanced by the use of both buds and open specimens of the same flower, so it is often a good idea to press them in both forms. But do not succumb to the temptation of trying to enjoy the beauty of the flowers on the plant for as long as possible, picking them for pressing only just before they fade or drop. This does not give good results.

Foliage also has to be picked at the right stage of development. The very young leaves of eccremocarpus, for example, and those of *Clematis montana* emerge from the press a striking black color. If picked when too mature, they turn out a much less inspiring flat green. Even grasses should be watched for the right stage – their delicate spikelets should be open, but not so far developed that they are ready to shed their seeds all over your designs.

Pick each species early in its season when the plants are lush and sappy – they will press far more successfully than those which appear later in the season.

Another important factor to consider is the weather. Damp is the flower-presser's main enemy: it encourages mildew. Specimens should therefore be collected on a dry day when any droplets of water from the showers of previous days are likely to have evaporated.

A collection of flowers sealed in an inflated plastic bag in order to maintain their freshness, as it was not possible to press them immediately.

ABOVE *Collecting celandines for pressing.*

ABOVE *Collecting forget-me-nots for pressing.*

The time of day is also important: a sunny afternoon is the best time of all. Even a fine morning may be damp with dew and, by early evening, some flowers will have closed for the night.

The final luxury of picking flowers locally is that it is practical to pick a few specimens at a time and to put them straight into the press before there is any possibility that their condition can deteriorate.

When traveling farther afield to collect flowers, it may be more difficult to ensure ideal conditions. However, the guidelines listed above still apply. The major problem is likely to be keeping the flowers fresh. If they have wilted by the time you arrive back home, it will be much more difficult to press them successfully.

Of the two major methods for maintaining freshness, one is to use a traveling press and with it to press the flowers as soon as possible after picking them, preferably in a sheltered spot. When you arrive home, the card and blotting paper 'sandwiches' with the flowers undisturbed inside, can be simply transferred to the main press. (Alternatively, if the traveling press is not likely to be required again for a while, you can put it under an additional weight and leave it exactly as it is.)

The second method of maintaining freshness is to carry around several airtight plastic bags. Collect the specimens directly into the bags – not too many in each or they may crush each other. When you have finished collecting, blow air into each bag, as if you were blowing up a balloon, and secure the top with a flexible tie. This air cushion serves to prevent the flowers from becoming crushed, over-heated or dried out. They should then arrive home – even many hours later – as fresh as when they were picked.

Remember to pick only perfect specimens. Pressing cannot improve a substandard bloom – and your designs can only be as beautiful as the individual flowers that make them up.

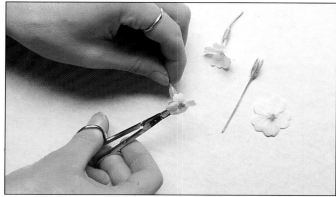

TOP *It is a simple matter to prepare buttercups for the press. Give them a good start by squeezing the centre of the open flower between thumb and finger, taking care to spread the petals evenly. Then place them, face downwards, on a layer of blotting paper or a page of your pressing book.*

ABOVE *Pressed specimens of flowers that need some preparation before successful pressing can take place. 1 Love-in-a-mist and 2 Saxifrage should both have their projecting seedboxes removed. The seed box behind the dog rose 3 also needs removing. The multi-flowered heads of elderflowers 4 must be separated into small sprays while hydrangea florets 5 must be pressed individually.*

T E C H N I Q U E S I N P R E S S I N G

The flowers and foliage collected will be of many different types, shapes and sizes. It may not always be possible to put them straight into a press without some form of preparation. Various techniques are involved.

The simplest flowers to press are those that are flat or like a shallow dish in shape. Buttercups are a good example of this type and can be persuaded easily into a new two-dimensional state.

Remove any part of a flower which might impair the appearance of the whole after it has been pressed. When flowers are to be pressed in the open form, for example, it is wise to remove stems from all but the sturdiest, in order to prevent them from bruising or deforming the petals under which they lie. For the same reason, certain parts of flowers – like the green calyx which sheathes the back of a primrose – are best removed.

Another reason for removing flower parts is to facilitate the transformation into the two-dimensional. Both love-in-a-mist (devil-in-the-bush) and saxifrage press well, once the seedboxes which project in front have been removed. The same can be said of the single dog rose after the careful removal of the seedbox from behind the flower.

TOP *It is a good idea to remove both the stem and the calyx of a primrose before pressing. The calyx might otherwise bruise the delicate petal under which it lies.*

ABOVE *Forget-me-not stems should be prepared for pressing by removing some of the individual flowers to prevent overcrowding. The spiral of buds at the top of the stem may also be pressed separately.*

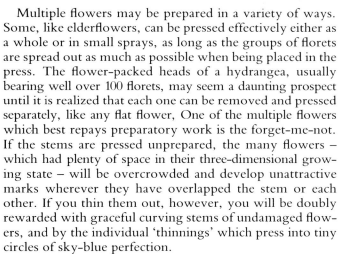

LEFT The three-dimensional daffodil can be sliced in two and pressed in profile.

ABOVE. All but the smallest rosebuds must be separated into individual petals before pressing. Press the green sepals for the later reconstruction of rosebuds.

Multiple flowers may be prepared in a variety of ways. Some, like elderflowers, can be pressed effectively either as a whole or in small sprays, as long as the groups of florets are spread out as much as possible when being placed in the press. The flower-packed heads of a hydrangea, usually bearing well over 100 florets, may seem a daunting prospect until it is realized that each one can be removed and pressed separately, like any flat flower, One of the multiple flowers which best repays preparatory work is the forget-me-not. If the stems are pressed unprepared, the many flowers – which had plenty of space in their three-dimensional growing state – will be overcrowded and develop unattractive marks wherever they have overlapped the stem or each other. If you thin them out, however, you will be doubly rewarded with graceful curving stems of undamaged flowers, and by the individual 'thinnings' which press into tiny circles of sky-blue perfection.

So far, I have considered only flowers that can be converted relatively easily to the two-dimensional. But what of truly three-dimensional flowers like daffodils, roses and carnations? It could be argued that these are best left alone by the flower-presser.

Daffodils can be pressed effectively by removing the seed-box and slicing through the trumpet, after which it is possible to press the two resulting 'profiles'. The same slicing technique can be used on very small rosebuds: larger ones, however, must be treated differently: remove the green sepals for separate pressing, and then carefully peel the delicate satin-smooth petals from the bud so that each one can be pressed individually. (When making rose designs later on, you can reconstruct 'buds' by building up layers of individual petals and using the centres of rock roses as false, but fairly true-to-life, middles.)

Carnations can be treated by the same 'separate petal' procedure. Their pressed petals make realistic 'buds' when used in combination with sections of the green sheath-like calyx.

It is always sensible to place only flowers of the same thickness in any one of the layer of the press. This eliminates the risk of putting the flatter ones under insufficient pressure, which could cause shrivelling or encourage mildew. But what if a single flower is itself of uneven thickness? This can sometimes be a problem. One occasionally sees daisies for example whose petals have become spiky because they have not been as heavily pressed as the middles. In the case of such small flowers this problem can usually be overcome by giving the yellow middles an extra firm squeeze before pressing. The solution is not so simple with the bigger daisies, or with other large daisy-type flowers you may want to press. These flowers have middles which are so significantly bulkier than their surrounding petals that it would be impossible to apply even pressure to the whole flower without the use of a 'collar'. This is a series of newspaper or blotting paper circles with the centers cut out to accommodate the thick middle; the correct number of layers of paper can be placed underneath the petals to even up the thickness.

As you gain experience you will develop all sorts of personal techniques for preparing particular flowers and other types of plant material. You may, for example, find it helpful to use a rolling pin to 'pre-press' a particularly thick stem of, say, *Clematis montana*. Alternatively, you may decide to slice it in two before pressing. You will also discover the exceptions to the 'rules' – particularly, perhaps, to the one which decrees that all plant material should be placed in the press as quickly as possible. Moss, for instance, almost invariably comes from a damp habitat and is therefore best left in a warm room for a few hours before pressing.

One final general point about preparation: although you are not necessarily considering the finer details of design at this stage, it is nevertheless helpful to keep the likely eventual designs in mind when you are arranging material in the press. Once the specimens are dried, they are more or less fixed in shape.

ABOVE A single daisy-type chrysanthemum being pressed by the 'collar' method.

ABOVE Clumps of moss should be allowed to dry out in a warm room for several hours before being separated into small pieces for pressing.

The Pressing Process: Hazards

The aim of this stage is to dry and flatten the flowers in such a way as to ensure that they come out of the press as bright and as beautiful as when they went in. There are various hazards from which they must now be protected. The three major ones are undue disturbance, mildew and incorrect pressure.

Once they have been prepared for pressing, flowers should not be disturbed any more than is absolutely necessary. This means that when the press is being filled, its layers of card and blotting paper must be carefully placed one on top of the other, so that the flowers do not move from the position in which you have set them, and none of the leaves or petals is accidentally folded over. Similar precautions should be taken when closing a pressing book: its pages should be gently rolled closed over the precious contents. You should, particularly in the early days, resist the temptation to 'see how they are getting on'. Partly pressed material is very limp and, once misshapen, is difficult to reshape correctly.

Mildew is the most serious risk at the pressing stage. It can be heartbreaking to open the press after several weeks and find everything inside covered with a damp grey mold. This should not happen if the necessary precautions are taken.

Make sure that flowers are under sufficient pressure. Pressing-books must be adequately weighted, and the wing-nuts of presses must be checked every day or two during the first week. This is because as the material in a press dries out, it becomes less bulky so that the nuts need tightening to maintain the pressure.

Keep your presses in a dry, airy place.

To avoid the spread of any mildew if it does occur, make sure that there is plenty of space between the flowers on

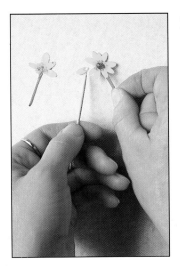

each layer, and that the layers themselves are well separated by corrugated card or several intervening pages.

Do not add any new, mosisture-laden material to a press or book already containing drying flowers.

In spite of my advice not to disturb the flowers unnecessarily, it is nevertheless sensible to inspect a few of them after a week or so to check for damp or mildew. If any is found, a more thorough check is indicated, during which you should throw away any even slightly mildewed specimens, and change damp blotting paper or pressing books.

The pressing process for subjects particularly prone to mildew, such as roses and carnations, may be best *startea* in any particularly warm dry place or airing-cupboard. But I would not recommend this for all flowers, or for any flowers for more than a few days. They can become dry and brittle if left too long.

Just as too little pressure can put flowers at risk, so over-pressing can also present a problem. It usually occurs only when a press containing layers of corrugated card is used. Such card is normally invaluable because its corrugations aid ventilation and help to prevent the spread of damp. Also its flexible thickness does much to maintain an even pressure on bulky subjects. If precautions are not taken, however, it can cause imperfections on delicate petals. Primroses, for example, pressed between single sheets of blotting paper sandwiched between this card, could emerge from the press with corrugations imprinted on their petals. You may feel happier using the book method for these tender specimens, but you can still use the press if you insert additional layers of blotting paper, or if perhaps you replace the card altogether with several thicknesses of newspaper.

A final note on pressing: it is worth mentioning that both blotting paper and pressing-books can be re-used indefinitely, if kept perfectly dry and free from mildew.

ABOVE A celandine with a missing petal being prepared with a good petal from another blemished specimen.

ABOVE Some specimens, like the individual flowers of forget-me-nots, have a tendency to stick to blotting paper. They can be teased off with a small, soft brush.

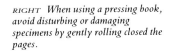

RIGHT When using a pressing book, avoid disturbing or damaging specimens by gently rolling closed the pages.

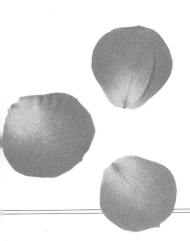

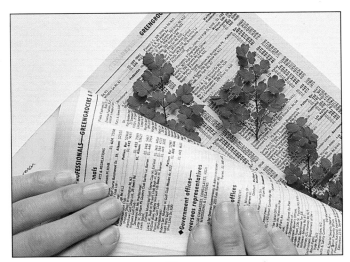

Pressing: Duration

Traditionally, the pressing process takes about six weeks – a slightly shorter time for small, dry specimens, and a little longer for those that are larger or more moisture-laden. A simple test of whether a flower is ready for use is to select a specimen still on its stem, and hold it up by the base of the stem. If it stands upright, it is ready; if it flops, it should be returned to the press for a little while longer.

At the height of summer, when flowers are at their most abundant, you may find you need a press for new material before its original contents have been in for long enough. It is reasonable, in such circumstances, to transfer the flowers carefully to well-weighted storage books at any time after the first ten days. If you do this, remember to label them clearly with the pressing date and not to use them in designs until the full six-week period is complete.

Other ways of shortening the time in the press involve the use of modern appliances. The aim of pressing flowers is to dry and flatten them so you might be forgiven for thinking that you could do this most efficiently with a domestic iron! In fact, if plant material is ever needed urgently (or an otherwise good flower has a creased petal), it is possible, with the iron on a low-heat setting, to press sturdy flowers or leaves between sheets of blotting paper. This process should be followed by a few days under pressure in a warm, dry place.

Now comes the pleasure of looking through the wealth of lovely pressed material from which you will soon be creating designs. If all has gone well, you will have many perfect two-dimensional representations of the original specimens in a variety of rich colors. Larkspur duplicate the shades of the growing flowers; the little annual phlox (Pride of Texas) undergo subtle color changes; the young leaves of eccremocarpus show an even more dramatic change.

It is sensible to discard any specimens that come out of the press discolored or faded, damaged or distorted. There will always be a small proportion of these, which would spoil your designs if used. (Do not, however, be too quick to throw away flowers that are only slightly damaged, for it may be possible to amalgamate two blemished blooms into one perfect specimen.)

It is worth mentioning here that although most flowers obligingly slide straight off their pressing backgrounds into their new storage accommodation, others need a little gentle persuasion before they will move. The tiny individual forget-me-nots, for example, have a tendency to stick to blotting paper, and each one needs to be patiently teased off with the soft tip of a fine brush. Fingernails or even tweezers may cause damage.

ABOVE A pressed daisy standing upright. It is now completely dry and ready for use.

RIGHT A collection of specimens just removed from the press on their blotting paper sheets.

BELOW Pressed specimens may be stored in books or cellophane-fronted bags. It is a good idea to label and index books, with dates, so that flowers are disturbed no more than is actually necessary.

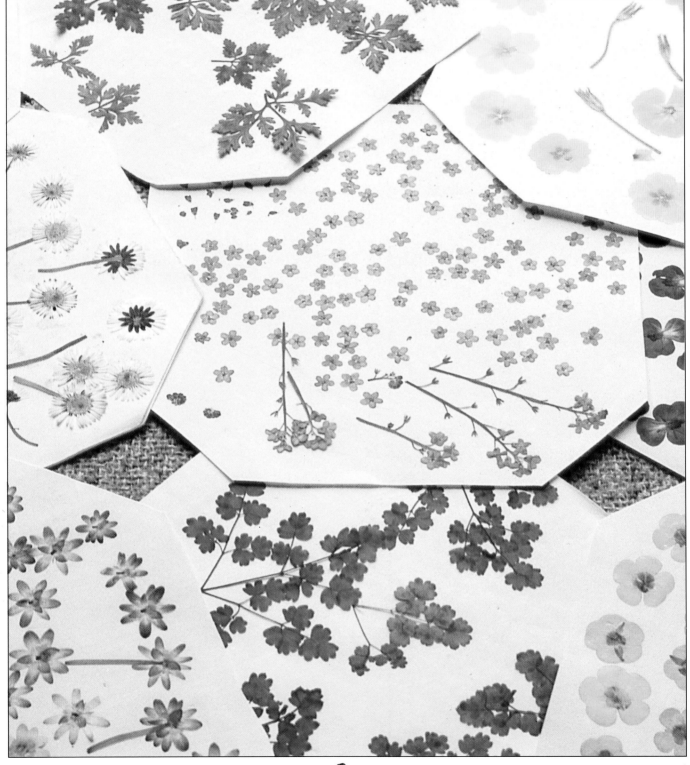

Storage

Once flowers have been pressed, they must remain perm–anently under some form of pressure, whether in storage or in their final settings. Only in this way will they remain in good condition; any exposure to air will put them at risk of reabsorbing moisture.

All pressed specimens are stored in a series of old telephone directories. These are excellent for the purpose because they are freely available, heavy enough to keep the flowers in good shape, and large enough not to overcrowd the specimens. Also, their absorbent pages deal with any poss–ible traces of remaining moisture. Another possibility is to store each type of flower in individual cellophane-fronted, paper-backed bags as described previously. Storage books and bags should, like presses, be kept in a dry, airy place and, if piled one on top of another, should be occasionally rearranged so that they are evenly ventilated.

Each type of flower should have its its own bag or section of book, and all the pressed material should be arranged in a logical and easy-to-find order. This is because the 'do-

Unprotected bookmarks. These simple and attractive designs were made with astrantia, buttercups and pansies each of which was carefully stuck down with several tiny areas of glue.

not-disturb-unnecessarily' rule remains as relevant as ever, and repeated searches through randomly-stored flowers for a particular specimen greatly increase the risk of damage.

It is best to keep separate books for miniature flowers, larger flowers, leaves, grasses, and so forth, and within each book the specimens can be arranged in the order in which they appear during the year. As a consequence of this, you will know that early flowers are usually to be found somewhere among the Collinses, while the mid-summer blooms live with the Joneses, and the autumn species with the Wilsons! This information is a little too vague, however, so at the beginning of each book keep a list of page numbers detailing exactly which flowers appear where. As an alternative to such a list, labels identifying flowers can be attached to the relevant pages or bags. These precautions should ensure that you can always find a partic-ular flower quickly and easily, and with the minimum of disturbance to the rest.

Great care is needed when removing specimens from bags and when replacing them if they are surplus to require-ments. Also, when turning the pages of storage books you should try to make sure that the contents do not slip towards the spine. If everything collects in this area, the book becomes misshapen – and so do the flowers.

These unprotected greetings cards are made in a similar way to the bookmarks. The pictures include saxifrage, buttercups and astrantia. Note how they can be made even more charming by the addition of a small design inside the card which reflects the main design.

Handling Pressed Flowers

You will be able to remove the sturdiest flowers from their storage books, and move them around on the design background, simply by using your fingers. When dealing with more delicate specimens, however, it may be helpful to use small tweezers to pick them up, and the tip of a fine brush to move them around on the design.

The method many people prefer for the most delicate flowers of all is to moisten the tip of your forefinger very slightly, by touching it just inside your lip. Apply gentle pressure to the flower to be picked up, which then usually sticks to your finger sufficiently well to allow you to transfer it to its new position. The great advantage of this technique is that you do not risk damaging your most fragile specimens by trying to get either fingers or tweezers underneath the petals.

Sticking Down

Once a design is in its setting, the glass – or whatever is used to protect your work – should be holding it so firmly in place, that nothing could possibly move. It is however, so difficult to get an 'unstuck' design into its setting without any of its components moving out of position, that it is almost essential to glue down every single piece.

This does not mean that the whole area of each flower has to be firmly stuck to its background. The smallest possible amount of adhesive should be applied, on the end

BELOW When sticking down a design, use a cocktail stick to apply a tiny spot of latex adhesive to the base of the thickest part of each flower.

BELOW Sticking down overlapping flowers.

ABOVE The best way of handling a delicate specimen is to apply gentle pressure to it with a slightly moist fingertip. The flower should then stick to your finger for long enough to enable you to move it into the desired position.

of a cocktail stick, to the back of the thickest part of each flower or leaf. Stems should have tiny spots of glue dotted along their length; fine materials like grasses and tendrils need stroking in only one or two places with a lightly glued stick.

You will soon find out if you are using too much glue, because it will show through delicate petals. Worse still, it may squeeze out from underneath and mark the background. If this happens with a latex adhesive, it is often possible to 'roll off' the offending glue by rubbing the marked area with a clean finger.

When you become experienced and are sure of the effect you are trying to create, you may choose to stick down each part of the design as you go along. If you are less experienced, or experimenting with new ideas, it is probably better to lay out the whole design before you stick any of it. Then, taking care not to disturb the surrounding flowers and leaves more than necessary, you can pick up each one separately and gently glue it into position. Where flowers overlap, you must, of course, stick down the underneath ones first.

ABOVE Snowdrops arranged with the attractive, white-lined spikes of a crocus plant.

BELOW Cowslips whose yellow flowers have turned green

1

6

3

Retaining Color

2

5

Color is not everything. The beauty of a pressed–flower design resides in far more than this, and wonderful effects can be achieved by using the subtlest and most muted of colors. The fact remains, however, that it is lovely to see flower pictures that capture the original brightness of nature. The question most frequently asked by people looking at pressed flowers is, 'How do you keep the colors so bright?' There is no 'magic' involved; if you press the right flowers and use the techniques outlined you have every chance of success.

Your responsibility for helping to retain colors does not end at the point where the flowers are safely in their settings. The position in which they are then displayed is important. No pressed–flower design should be constantly exposed to direct sunlight (so do not stand paperweights on sunny windowsills). Remember also that moisture can continue to be a problem so a room like a damp conservatory could be a disastrous place to hang a flower picture.

There is, of course, one means by which it is possible to make certain that flowers retain their color. This is the technique, recommended by several books on the subject, of coloring flowers permanently with poster paints. Decide for yourself on this matter. To some, the hard, artificial colors of paint fail to blend with the subtler natural shades of flowers. If a flower is going to lose color to the point at which it will no longer be attractive, perhaps it would be better not to use it at all.

When dealing with the fine translucent petals of such flowers as the primrose, putting one, or even two, additional flowers on top of the original one will intensify its color. A daisy with a bright yellow middle but thin petals can be superimposed on one with a discoloured middle but beautiful pink-edged petals. Similar 'tricks' can be employed with foliage. Except when making 'botanical pictures', you could substitute leaves which are more attractive to keep color

THIS PAGE Color testers and the lessons to be learnt from them. *1 Forget-me-nots, spiraea (both white and pink), saxifrage and the veined petals of the ballerina geranium all keep their color well. The alpine phlox and the purple lobelia (as opposed to the blue one) do not. 2 Montbretia buds and hypericum keep color beautifully. 3 All the flowers in this frame (blue lobelia, heuchera, lady's mantle, astrantia and the heather florets) have proved reliable. 4 This frame shows that the larkspur and delphinium (right) are better color-keepers than the love-in-a-mist (left). 5 The hardy fuschsia is seen to keep color reliably. 6 The 'everlasting' helipterum and anaphalis included here are still bright as is the darker of the rock roses.*

It is apparent from these color testers that, while foliage which presses black or silver maintains its original color, almost all green foliage fades.

4

RIGHT AND ABOVE Ways of improving color naturally. *Three primroses have been superimposed here to intensify their delicate color, and interest is added to the large daisy by the superimposition of a slightly smaller pink-edged specimen.*

better than a particular flower's own leaves. When working with snowdrops, for example, you can use the similar but prettier white-lined crocus spikes.

The whole subject of color retention in pressed flowers is fascinating, and the only way to study it satisfactorily is to observe the various changes which take place over the years. This requires patience, of course, but you will, in time, be rewarded by knowing which flowers are going to retain their colors most reliably.

A series of 'color testers', comprising a wide variety of flowers mounted in frames, will show you what the passing years do to them. The flowers and foliage fall into three categories: those that keep their color well; those that pale down but are still beautiful enough to be worth using against the right background; and those that, regretfully, are not worth pressing again. One of the greatest surprises with respect to a bizarre color-change was the once limpid yellow cowslips: they are now bright green!

AESTHETIC PRINCIPLES

O nce you have a collection of good pressed material, you are ready to proceed with confidence to the design stage. Sadly, however, this is just the point at which many people come to a standstill. The design section of books on flower-pressing with their references to 'contour', 'balance', 'harmony' and other technicalities can be somewhat daunting to a beginner. Therefore what follows is an absolutely practical approach. Of course, this is not the only way to begin, but it should help you to build up confidence as you progress. Try working through the following steps, using your own choice of flowers, introducing variations whenever you wish, and abandoning my suggestions altogether at the point at which you find your own style.

Start Small, Start Simple

Choose a small setting and be prepared, at this stage, to rely entirely on the beauty of one individual flower to create the design. Choose your flower with care, for you will not get away with such complete simplicity unless it is a perfect specimen, and unless it is sufficiently intricate or visually interesting to satisfy the eye. Background color and texture are all important, the use of fabric is recommended for the additional interest it can provide. (Try placing your flower

THIS PAGE Start small, start simple. *Four 'designs' each relying on the beauty of the individual flowers to create the finished effect. 1 Love-in-a-mist 2 Burnet Saxifrage 3 Astrantia 4 Wild Carrot.*

1

2

3

4

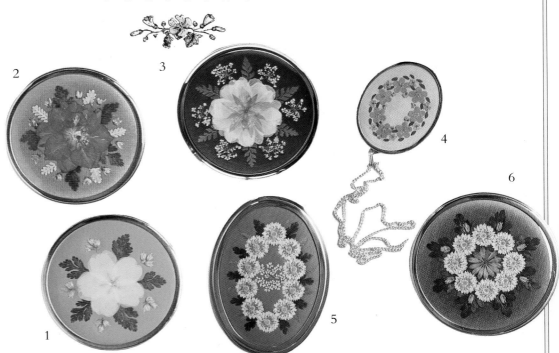

Add a little embellishment. *Foliage and extra small flowers have been added to the main central flower in each of these designs. 1 Primrose with golden rod and herb Robert foliage. 2 Larkspur with heather and both silver and green foliage. 3 Limnanthes with cow parsley and fern.*

Make a symmetrical design. *Use a selection of regularly shaped flowers and rely on symmetry to produce an attractive effect. The two larger designs 5 and 6 are based on the anaphalis, the round one (6) has the underside of a regularly shaped astrantia for its centerpiece and the oval centre is earthnut. The pendant design 4 is made of forget-me-nots and elderflowers.*

on a variety of different backgrounds to decide which one enhances it most.) Finally, try to ensure that your work is technically perfect, for a badly positioned flower, a roughly cut-out piece of fabric, or a single spot of unwanted glue can mar simple designs.

An ideal flower for this purpose is the astrantia. With its tiny flowers and surrounding pointed bracts, it needs no further embellishment.

Another particularly suitable candidate for the simple approach is love-in-a-mist (devil-in-a-bush), with its dark green central stamens and fine misty-green foliage that surrounds the flower. A little judicious rearrangement might be necessary if this foliage is not evenly spread, but basically it is still the simple beauty of the flower which does the design work.

The lacy flower-heads of the Umbellifers are also sufficiently intricate to stand alone.

You should as you gain experience succeed in making larger and more elaborate pressed flower pictures. But for sheer simple beauty, you may never make anything to surpass these small, one-flower 'designs' in which the patience, care and technique are yours but the art is all nature's.

Add a Little Embellishment

Begin again with a single central flower, but this time, use a slightly larger setting and add some pieces of foliage, radiating from the centre. Then introduce some other tiny flowers in colors that blend both with the central specimen and with the background.

In the simplest of the three designs shown, two primroses have been placed one on top of the other to intensify their pale color. The shape of the petals has been allowed to suggest the position of the five pieces of herb Robert leaf, and three single florets of golden rod, whose deeper color blends with the pale primroses, have been arranged in each of the spaces thus created.

The *Limnanthes* design on the darker green also uses two superimposed central flowers, this time with the pale green leaves of a delicate fern in the shape of a six-pointed star, and the heads of cow parsley, making a dainty space-filler.

The design using the central larkspur is the most complex, using two contrasting types of foliage, with the pink heather florets as space-fillers.

Make a Symmetrical Design

Having made some semi-regular designs based on a single central flower, you will want to progress to more complex work. One way to introduce this is to try something completely symmetrical. Pressed-flower pictures should always be balanced and in proportion, but they certainly need not be symmetrical. Indeed, it would be very limiting to make only regular designs. These can, however, be beautiful, and the reason for considering them here is that it is not difficult, even for a beginner, to think out a symmetrical design that works well. This does not mean that they are easy to make from a technical point of view. They demand quite as much care and patience in choosing and positioning flowers and foliage, which must be carefully selected for their regularity of both size and shape.

Try working with the beautifully regular anaphalis (pearly everlasting), together with the leaves of herb Robert. If these are unobtainable, you may be able to find enough regular specimens of the equally attractive common daisy. Among the smaller flowers that work well in symmetrical designs are forget-me-nots, saxifrage, spiraea and elder-flower. You will see from the examples that this sort of design succeeds equally well in round or oval settings. It could also be easily adapted to fit a rectangular frame.

Use Nature As Designer

You should by now be beginning to think about making 'free' designs. A lovely way of doing this – if you are still feeling unsure of yourself – is to use nature itself as designer. What could be more simply effective than an oval picture, backed on green velvet, depicting snowdrops as they appear in a spring garden, or the graceful curves of heather as it blows on moorlands?

This sort of design looks deceptively simple, but be prepared for it to take quite as long to make as something more intricate, because it is so important that it looks just

BELOW Use nature as designer. These simple designs show snowdrops and heather just as they grow naturally.

RIGHT Four ideas are suggested by the rectangular outline of these greetings cards. The first follows half the shape of the frame in an L-shaped design, the largest flower set in the right-angle of the L, and the smallest flowers and dainty foliage softening the outline. On the second card, the focal flower is placed centrally, towards the base of the rectangle, the delicate fern and tiny heuchera leading the eye upwards and outwards. The third card displays a regular design with the pink-edged central daisy claiming immediate attention. The fourth design 'starts' in the top left-hand corner, from where the pendant fuchsias fall to focus attention on the middle of the card. The fuchsia stamens and forget-me-nots then trail away to lead the eye downwards.

right. Snowdrops should be the correct size in relation to each other, their heads hanging at natural angles; and the shapes of the heather stems should look as if they really are growing together. It may be necessary to look through most of your specimens of a particular flower before you find a perfectly natural-looking group, but the end result should make the time spent well worthwhile.

If you are a botanist at heart, you may well decide that this is the type of flower-work for you. You could then go on to make a variety of botanical pictures of individual species, using both open flowers and buds, together with the correct leaves, and possibly a sliced-through seed-pod. You might even include a washed and pressed section of root. As a final touch, you might want to inscribe the work with the common and Latin names of the flowers.

Balance

Although it is not necessary for a design to be regular in any way, it must be balanced. Balance is not always easy to achieve, and one occasionally looks at a picture, knowing that something is wrong although it is not always clear exactly what. A good technique for diagnosing this sort of problem is to turn the picture round and look at it at a different angle. Quite often, a fault that eluded you when the picture was the right way up becomes glaringly obvious when it is upside down.

A good exercise in creating balance is to make a picture entirely from leaves. Leaf pictures are more adaptable than flower designs for this 'all ways round' viewing. Try making one and checking its balance from every angle.

Originality

Sooner or later, you will want to create something original. The joy of working with flowers is that you will certainly be able to do this. If you are artist enough to sketch out ideas for designs, either mentally or on paper, so much the better. But if, like me, you are unable to plan in this way, it is still possible to make designs that are both attractive and original. All you have to do is to allow the flowers themselves to make the suggestions. There is no need to start with a clear idea of the sort of design you want to make. You can simply take some carefully pressed flowers and foliage, and place them on a background color that enhances their beauty, inside a frame or mount that suits both flowers and background. Then all you have to do is move them around until they suggest ideas.

ABOVE *These three designs each use the same flowers and foliage (buttercups, cow parsley and herb Robert) and the same background color to illustrate three different arrangements in a round frame. The first is a crescent-shaped design which follows the frame outline. The second has a central focal point made up of three main flowers. In the third, the flowers are arranged more naturally as if growing.*

Style and Representation

There is a sense in which there are as many different styles as there are pressed-flower artists. And the style of even one individual is likely to keep changing and developing as time passes. It is possible, nevertheless, to identify a number of general stylistic areas. You might like to try your hand at each of these.

The modern style is characterized by its simplicity and concentration on the individual flower. It often uses only one main flower type in any design, together with one or two smaller species which serve to soften the outline and complement the color of the main blooms. These designs generally have an 'open' appearance, using space to ensure that the individual beauty of each flower is clearly seen.

In contrast to this, the more traditional style commonly uses a mass of overlapping blooms to create a total effect, rather than focusing attention on individual flowers. Many pictures of this sort contain a large number of different species, and are often big enough to accommodate large specimens. The overall effect of this traditional work is full, heavy and grand.

Representational designs are different again. They can vary greatly, ranging from complex and intricately-worked pictures to 'designs' which seem to present themselves ready-made.

There are many beautiful examples of complex representational work depicting such subjects as elegant ladies with sumptuous gowns, fashioned entirely from overlapping delphinium petals; graceful swans, brought to life from the feathery silver leaves of cineraria and silverweed; and the most exquisitely-worked landscapes.

Some of the most original representational work is that which uses seeds in all their subtle varieties of color, texture and shape to make the most charming and realistic pictures of birds.

It is obvious that an enormous amount of loving care has gone into making these pictures. The outline of the bird is first sketched on to the background card, after which the eyes and beak are fixed into position. Then a small area of glue is applied directly to the card and each seed is carefully placed in position, working from the bottom upwards to ensure that the 'feathers' overlap realistically.

It sometimes happens that simple representations of such subjects as butterflies, birds and trees offer themselves straight from the pages of pressing books. A single petal has only to fall from the five-petalled St John's wort – and there is a 'butterfly' with stamen antennae. If two petals fall from the beautifully-veined ballerina geranium, four 'wings' are again revealed (and, if you are lucky, there will also be two visible sections of calyx in the right position for anten-

ABOVE *In this seed picture, the tawny owl is fashioned mainly from hogweed seeds, with pear-pips (seeds) for eyes, the curved seeds of marigold for 'eyebrows' and cosmos daisies for claws.*

RIGHT *Simply made birds. 1 A 'swan' made from a cranesbill seed pod and silverweed leaves. 2 A Christmas robin with a cherry tree body and clematis tail. 3 More cherry leaf birds in flight.*

nae). It is only one step from this to selecting four suitably-proportioned *Clematis montana* leaves, and making a butterfly with an oaty grass spikelet for a body and fuchsia stamens for antennae.

It is not only insects that 'appear' in this way. The aptly-named cranesbill seed-pod simply asks to be made into a bird's head and neck, and looks effective with the feathery leaves of silverweed forming a swan-like body. Other birds 'grow' on the flowering cherry tree. You have only to look at the feathery outlines of its foliage to imagine a group of birds in flight, and those of its leaves which obligingly turn red on one 'breast' in autumn, make delightful robins when given a seed eye, leaf wing and fanciful clematis seed tail.

You will also discover 'trees' in the pages of pressing books. It is a simple matter to incorporate the lush green fern 'species' into summer landscapes, and those with the bare silver 'branches' into wintry scenes. (And whatever the season, a few grass seed 'birds' could fly around the treetops.)

LEFT The designs on the lids of the top two colored porcelain boxes are fairly similar, but each one is mounted on a different-colored fabric to match the base of the box. Quite different effects can be achieved by interchanging the lids. In the pairing picture the pink lid has been exchanged with the green one. Now the green foliage on the pink velvet is highlighted by its new green base, and the pink heather florets on the green background come to life because of the pink underneath them.

Color

There are three color elements to be considered in relation to any design: the color of the flowers; of the background; and of the frame or setting. Vastly different effects can be achieved by different combinations of these three elements. One of the delights of working with flowers is experimenting with them.

Everyone has different ideas on how to choose flower colors. Successful pictures range from those which imitate the summer herbaceous border in presenting a riot of mixed colors, to those which use the most muted of shades.

Choosing background color is largely an artistic decision, but it has one technical aspect. Most pressed flowers lose some color of the years and some fade relatively quickly. It is therefore inadvisable to use very pale backgrounds unless there is a good reason to be confident about the color fastness of the flowers being used. When – as in the case of celandines – you know that they will lose much of their brilliance during the first year, choose a strong background color. Experiment, placing the flowers on different backgrounds to find out which combinations best please you.

This design of buttercups, golden rod and montbretia, and acer leaves follows the shape of the oval frame.

Such experiments should continue when you introduce the third element: the frame or setting. Ask yourself what you are looking for – harmony or contrast? And which parts of the picture are you trying to emphasize?

Choice of Frame

The oval frame is perhaps the most attractive for flower work. It is well proportioned for use with 'growing flower' designs that follow the contour of the frame. These are not difficult to make because the shape of the frame can actually act as a guide when you are arranging the flowers. First decide upon a focal point – the spot that is going to attract the eye first. This is usually towards the base of the picture, and often consists of the largest flowers or group of flowers. It may be central or slightly off-set, but in either case, the eye should rest on this point, before being led upwards and outwards towards the smaller, lighter flowers and foliage which follow the curve of the frame.

Round frames can also be used effectively with designs which follow their contours, but like ovals they are versatile enough to be used in other ways as well.

Rectangular frames or outlines offer similar scope for design shapes.

USEFUL FLOWERS FOR PRESSING

The fruits and vegetables that we are now able to buy are increasingly international and the same is true of the flowers in florists and nurseries. Cultivated flowers are invariably descended from wild flowers or are actually wild flowers from another part of the world. For example many cultivated lobelias, montbretias and heathers grown in northern temperate countries originated in South Africa; fuchsias have similarly been exported from New Zealand, and the lovely *Helipterum roseum* and several other everlasting flowers from Australia; the flowering currant, heuchera, the *Limnanthes,* larkspur, phlox, hydrangea and golden rod are from North America.

If you are unfamiliar with some of the flowers listed below, identify similar members of the same plant family that grow near you and try pressing them instead. Violets and pansies (Violaceae), vetches (Leguminosae), heathers (Ericaceae) and daisies (Compositae) are all members of families that have a worldwide distribution. (The Composites that I have included in this section should be pressed using the collar method if they are to be used whole.)

In North America, there are many different species of viola. Perhaps the most immediately attractive is the fern-leaved violet, *Viola vittata,* which is rather like *Viola tricolor.* You might also try some of the large number of North American pea plants (Leguminosae) and any heathers that grow in your area. The most obvious Composite to try is *Gaillardia pulchella,* otherwise known as Indian blanket, or, more descriptively, firewheels. Both the swamp rose and the prairie rose should press satisfactorily.

In New Zealand and Australia, there is again considerable potential in the vetch and viola families. In the absence of native heathers, try intead the pink *Epacis impressa* and the smaller-flowered white *E. microphylla.* Any everlasting flower flat enough to press is also a candidate for attention, so it would be well worth trying small specimens of the strawflower or yellow paper daisy, *Helichrysum bracteatum.*

Cultivated Flowers: Spring

ALYSSUM

(Alyssum saxatile)

This is the sweet-smelling yellow alyssum which is often grown together with aubretia. It is not a marvelous color-keeper, but is too pretty to pass over completely. Press its minute, round buds and tiny, just open, flowers.

SPIRAEA

(Spiraea argula)

A shrub that produces large numbers of tiny white flowers on slender arching stems. Each flower should be snipped off and pressed separately. A little later on in the season look out for *S. bumalda,* which produces clusters of crimson flowers.

POACHED EGG PLANT

(Limnanthes douglasii)

A quickly spreading hard annual, producing dish-shaped flowers which are easy to press and very attractive. Putting one or more directly on top of another intensifies their delicate color.

HEUCHERA

(Heuchera sanguinea)

One of the most useful small flowers, and one of the best red ones for keeping color. The bell-shaped blooms grow many to a stem. Pick them when the lower flowers are fully out and the top ones still in bud, for then the stem is spread enough to be pressed whole.

ANEMONE

(Anemone blanda)

A delicate daisy-like flower with blue or mauve petals surrounding a yellow middle. Choose only those with the deepest color.

PRIMULA

(Primula spp.)

There are many different species of this valuable flower, some of which have a bloom on each stem, whereas others grow in clusters. Most of them are potential 'pressers' and it is well worth while experimenting. The yellow and orange flowers usually press true, while the reds and purples darken. It is advisable to remove the green calyx and to trim off that part of the back of the flower which would otherwise lie behind one of the delicate petals and mark it.

FLOWERING CURRANT

(Ribes sanguineum)

Another spring-flowering shrub, valuable for its small bell-shaped flowers which hang in clusters. Press buds and flowers separately.

DAFFODIL

(Narcissus minimus)

In spite of their three-dimensional shape, ordinary daffodils can be pressed by the usual method. It is probably simpler, however, to stick to those varieties of the extensive *Narcissus* family which can be pressed whole. These include the miniature daffodil, named above, which is small enough to be pressed in profile, and the lovely narcissus, 'Soleil d'or', which has several golden flowers on each stem. The trumpet sections of these flowers are relatively flat and will, if you make a few small snips in them, lie against the outer petals so that you can press them open.

FORGET-ME-NOT

(Myosotis alpestris)

Invaluable, and well worth the trouble of snipping off some of the flowers for separate pressing. This creates uncrowded stems which also press well. The spiral of buds at the top of each stem is particularly attractive.

SAXIFRAGE

(Saxifraga urbium)

This produces sprays of small pink flowers on each stem. Flowers should be pressed separately after the removal of the projecting seedboxes. This is a painstaking process, but you will be rewarded with little pink circles, spotted with deep red, which look delightful in miniature designs together with forget-me-nots. Try also the larger-flowered saxifrages which grow one to a stem. The rose-colored ones press beautifully, producing pink, almost translucent petals.

Cultivated Flowers: Summer

LOVE-IN-A-MIST OR DEVIL-IN-THE-BUSH

(Nigella damascena)

Not such a reliable color-keeper but so beautiful, with its blue flower-head surrounded by fine misty green foliage, that it is still a good choice if mounted on a strong background color. Remove the seedbox before pressing.

LADY'S MANTLE

(Alchemilla mollis)

Tiny yellow-green star-shaped flowers grow on intricately branched heads. Press these in small sprays – but not too soon. Let the heads open out a little, or the pressed spray will look solid and lumpy.

ROSE

(Rosa spp.)

I have been surprised to read in more than one book on this craft that pressed roses 'always turn beige or brown.' This need not be so if the petals are pressed individually and are taken from mature buds rather than from open flowers. In the case of miniature roses, it is possible to avoid pressing the petals separately by slicing the buds in two, and pressing each half in profile. The smallest rose of all is the much loved *Rosa farreri persetosa*. This is a single variety, so the tiny buds can actually be pressed whole. They look delightful in simple designs which also use their miniature leaves.

ROCK ROSE

(Helianthemum nummularium)

This flowers profusely in the summer sunshine, in a wide variety of bright colors. The petals are fragile but, handled with care, should press perfectly. They are best gathered early in the day for, later on, the petals have a tendency to drop. Do not discard these 'bare' middles, however, because they make realistic centers for reconstructed roses.

LOBELIA

(Lobelia erinus)

Another 'true blue' color-keeper. Pick only a few at a time for its petals curl quickly.

Gypsophila or Babies' breath

(Gypsophila paniculata)

These sprays of tiny white flowers are very useful as delicate 'space fillers' to soften the outline of designs.

Larkspur

(Delphinium consolida)

More useful than its perennial relative, this annual has an even bigger range of colors which are bright, press 'true', and do not fade. Could you ask for more?

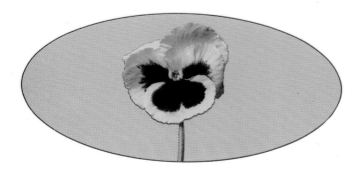

Pansy

(Viola tricolor hortensis)

These are found in many different sizes and colors. (Yellow flowers keep their color particularly well.) My preference is for the smaller ones and those with the most defined 'faces'.

Grandmother's pincushion

(Astrantia carniolica)

The true flowers of this interesting plant are tiny, but the surrounding bracts look like the petals of a larger flower. These bracts may be white and green, pink or a maroon-red. Their pointed shape gives them a geometric appearance, like the points of a compass.

Delphinium

(Delphinium elatum)

This is a tall perennial with colors varying from pale blue to deep mauve. It proudly contradicts the fallacy that blue flowers do not keep their color. (I have seen pictures of pages taken from a scrapbook over 100 years old in which the delphiniums are still blue!) Each flower on the stem should be pressed individually, but may still be rather large for many designs. If this is the case, wait for smaller flowers on the side-shoots, or consider pressing the petals separately.

Clary

(Salvia horminum)

This is another plant with insignificant flowers whose beauty is in its bracts. These are pink and purple and keep color well. They can be used in designs as the 'petals' of imaginary flowers.

PERUVIAN LILY

(Alstroemeria aurantiaca)

This lovely perennial, which grows in a variety of colors, is a good example of a three-dimensional flower whose individual petals are so beautiful that it is really worth while pressing them separately, prior to reconstructing them into imaginary two-dimensional flowers. Unfortunately these flowers are more frequently seen in florists' shops than in gardens – but perhaps this is something we should try to change, for they are not difficult to grow and the species named above is hardy.

PHLOX OR PRIDE OF TEXAS

(Phlox drummondii)

The short annual species of phlox, each stem of which bears many flowers in dense heads. Pick the florets singly and trim off the backs. The various colors undergo subtle changes during pressing.

ST JOHN'S WORT

(Hypericum elatum)

This shrub species produces masses of small, yellow, dish-shaped flowers, measuring about 1in (2.5cm) across and having a lovely central boss of golden stamens. Remove the seedbox before pressing. The stamens are even more spectacular on the shorter but larger-flowered *H. calycinum,* known as the rose of Sharon or Aaron's beard.

HYDRANGEA

(Hydrangea spp.)

Many species of this plant are excellent for pressing. The pinks, blues, and even the underdeveloped greens press well once the florets have been separated from the densely-flowering heads.

FUCHSIA

(Fuchsia magellanica)

The flowers of this bushy shrub are smaller and less moisture-laden than those of most of its exotic relatives. These are the qualities which make it the hardiest of the fuchsias and the best for pressing. Press the lovely pendant flowers in profile, leaving them on their curving stems and taking care to arrange the petals evenly. The scarlet stamens are so striking that you might occasionally choose to use them separated from the flower (for instance as butterfly antennae).

MONTBRETIA

(Crocosmia x crocosmiiflora)

Pick these graceful curving stems when most of the flowers are still in bud. They then retain their deep, orange color. Any of the trumpet-shaped flowers which are already out may be pressed separately, open or in profile.

Cultivated Flowers: Autumn and Winter

HEATHER

(Erica carnea)

The various winter-flowering heathers provide wonderful splashes of color at a time when this is otherwise in short supply. The pink varieties are particularly attractive. The flower spikes can be pressed whole, but what comes out of the press tend to be too solid-looking to use as it is. So discard the woody stems and spiky leaves, which usually drop off anyway, and use only the tiny bright pink flowers.

SNOWDROP

(Galanthus nivalis)

Use only the 'single-skirted' varieties and press in bud or profile. Do not try to press them open because this looks unnatural. Consider using them with the spiky white-lined leaves of the crocus.

GOLDEN ROD

(Solidago spp.)

Remove the curved plumes of tiny golden flowers from the tall stems. These may then be used whole, or separately for miniature designs.

Everlastings

Anaphalis, sea lavender and helipterum, are all of the 'ever-lasting' type more usually seen in three-dimensional dried-flower arrangements. They are more or less dry when picked, and need only to be hung up for a week or two in a warm, airy place to complete the process. They then need pressing very briefly just to flatten them, and they can subsequently be relied upon to retain color for years. The best everlasting specimens for pressing are, of course, those which are not too bulky.

SEA LAVENDER OR STATICE

(Limonium sinuatum)

This grows in a variety of bright colors. Press each of the florets separately.

ANAPHALIS OR PEARLY EVERLASTING

(Anaphalis yedoensis)

Clusters of pearly white flowers grow on a single stem. When they are dry, remove the seed heads from the middle of each flower to reveal the beautifully detailed, green-centered faces. Press each flower separately.

HELIPTERUM

(Helipterum roseum)

A beautiful pink daisy-like flower with papery-dry petals.

Wild Flowers

Never pick rare flowers. Never pick common flowers from places where they are scarce or protected. Remember that if you pick all this year's crop, there will be no seeds for next year. However abundant the flowers may be, never pick more than you need.

Fortunately, most of the best wild flowers for pressing are the very common ones. There are, however, one or two exceptions. It is now unusual, for example, to come across large numbers of primroses or heartsease (wild pansies) in the countryside.

It is even more important with wild flowers to have some idea about when to expect them because, unlike their cultivated counterparts, many wild flowers may be too far away to present a daily visual reminder that now is the time to gather them, and some of them have a relatively short season.

Coltsfoot

(Tussilago farfara)

This is the only one of the dandelion-type flowers to press satisfactorily because, unlike the others, it has a flat middle. It is therefore easy to spread the surrounding spiky 'petals' evenly. Again, it is worth considering using its equally attractive underside.

Bird's foot trefoil

(Lotus corniculatus)

An attractive meadow flower, best pressed in bud because the deep yellow buds are richer in color and sometimes, if you are lucky, tipped with red. This is a member of the vetch family, or Leguminosae, many of whose members, yellow or purple, are well worth considering for pressing.

Celandine

(Ranunculus ficaria)

These brilliant yellow starry flowers open their glossy petals to reflect the spring sunshine. They will pale down after a year or so to a lemony-cream color, but they are so beautiful in form that, if mounted against a dark background, they will still be attractive.

Elderflower

(Sambucus nigra)

These frothy, cream flower-heads have many florets to a stem. Heads may be pressed complete or in sprays. Used individually or in clusters in a design, the creamy-beige flowers add delicacy to your work.

DOG ROSE

(Rosa canina)

This charmingly simple wild rose is unlike its lusher, fuller-petalled garden relatives in that it can be pressed whole. Remove the seedbox from behind the flower.

COW PARSLEY

(Anthriscus sylvestris)

This is just one of the many useful species of the Umbellifer family. Others to look out for are fool's parsley, earthnut, burnet saxifrage, rough chervil and wild carrot. All have branched umbels, each topped with 'rays' or clusters of tiny flowers. To make a representation of such intricate structures in paint, embroidery or lace would indeed be work for a patient artist. But nature makes it easy for the flower-presser by offering us this family of plants, the different members of which adorn the countryside throughout the late spring and summer. Press whole umbels or separate rays.

HEATHER

(Calluna vulgaris)

This common wild variety is, perhaps, preferable to its stiffer cultivated counterparts. It grows on moorland and you can almost see the wind in the graceful curves of its stems. Its foliage, too, is attractive and does not drop.

DAISY

(Bellis perennis)

This most indispensable of all wild flowers certainly lives up to its Latin name, for not only does it recur profusely year after year, it also has a long season, in many areas appearing before most flowers we would particularly associate with spring, and continuing to bloom well into the autumn. Moreover, it is an ideal candidate for pressing. The best specimens are those with pink-edged petals (probably the result of cross-pollination with the cultivated varieties).

BUTTERCUP

(Ranunculus acris)

Beautiful and easy to press, buttercups grow abundantly in many areas. Avoid roadside flowers if possible, for they are usually dusty. *R. repens* is the equally attractive creeping buttercup.

Foliage

It is possible to make effective designs using leaves only, but though flower pictures without foliage may be pretty, they are bound to look unnatural – for where can flowers ever be seen growing in the absence of greenery?

It follows, therefore, that it is necessary to press a good selection of leaves. As with flowers there are some which press better than others and some general guidelines may be given regarding which these are. Types of leaves to avoid are the fleshy ones, like those of African violet; needles, like those of pine or many of the cultivated heathers; and thick evergreens, such as laurel, which refuse to dry out properly. Most other types of leaves press successfully, and the choice depends on finding specimens that are manageably small, interesting in shape and attractive in color.

HERB ROBERT

(Geranium robertianum)

The small purple flowers of this plant are fairly ordinary, but the beautifully-shaped, slightly hairy leaves are invaluable. They are often made even more attractive in the latter part of the year by a tinge of red.

EARTHNUT

(Conopodium majus)

Many members of the Umbellifer family have delicate leaves which press well. This is the most dainty, especially when gathered in the spring, before the white flowers appear. Press as soon as possible after picking, or the leafy sprays tend to wilt and close up.

COMMON MEADOW RUE

(Thalictrum flavum)

The tiny yellow flowers are insignificant but the leaves are beautifully angular. Press both the bright green leaves of midsummer and those which turn yellow as the plant approaches the end of its season.

SILVERWEED

(Potentilla anserina)

This is another indispensable plant, whose feather-edged leaves are grey-green on top and silver underneath. They can be used whole in large designs and are equally beautiful when segmented into smaller pieces. Silver-leaved plants are generally useful for the attractive variation they bring to designs and because they do not change color. Cultivated cineraria and pyrethrum also offer particularly beautiful silver leaves.

VIRGINIA CREEPER

(Parthenocissus quinquefolia)

These beautifully shaped leaves are at their best in their glorious autumn colors.

PYRETHRUM

(Chrysanthemum/Pyrethrum ptarmica folium)

Also known as silver feather, this plant has intricately-shaped leaves which can be used whole or separated into small sections for use in miniature designs.

CLEMATIS

(Clematis montana)

The young leaves turn a striking black when pressed.

ECCREMOCARPUS OR CHILEAN GLORY FLOWER

(Eccremocarpus scaber)

A useful annual climber, whose tubular orange flowers are best left alone but whose interestingly-shaped leaves also turn black on pressing.

COMMON IVY OR ENGLISH IVY

(Hedera helix)

Press the smaller leaves of the dark green varieties which keep color better than the variegated ones.

CINERARIA

(Cineraria maritima)

The 'Silver dust' variety has delicate fern-like leaves.

The Leaves of Trees

MAPLE

(Acer spp.)

all the members of the large acer family of trees and shrubs are grown for their ornamental foliage, and produce a variety of beautiful shapes and colors.

BEECH

(Fagus sylvatica)

Both the green and copper varieties are best pressed in spring. The young leaves of the copper beech give an autumn feel to designs.

OAK OR ENGLISH OAK

(Quercus pedunculata)

Press the immature leaves in spring time.

SUMACH

(Rhus spp.)

Best picked in autumn, when the leaves turn brilliant orange or scarlet. Look for smaller leaves on the creeping suckers.

FLOWERING CHERRY

(Prunus spp.)

There are many varieties of these lovely trees. The leaves of most of them are beautiful in autumn and best collected just before they drop. Their lovely colors, shape and feathery outline make these leaves perfect for Christmas card 'robins.'

Other Plant Material

SEEDS

The loveliest are probably the feathery whirls produced by many of the different varieties of clematis. The winged seeds of the sycamore maple *(Acer pseudoplatanus)* can also be used to make similar simple representations of moths' wings. Some 'natural artists' work only in this medium.

FERNS

Many types of fern press satisfactorily. Three that are used regularly are the delicate maiden-hair fern (*Adiantum capillus-veneris*) with its lovely sprays of green, and two bigger ferns: the common bracken or brake (*Pteridium aquilinum*) and the prettier hay-scented buckler fern (*Dryopteris aemula*). Pick young fronds, but consider splitting them into more manageable sizes before pressing.

GRASSES

Most grasses press well because they are fairly dry to start with. The delicate grasses are perhaps the most useful because they help to achieve a lovely soft outline when used for filling the spaces around a design. But try to press a variety of specimens: green and brown; straight and curved; solid and feathery.

SEED-PODS

There are several of these which can be attractively used in two-dimensional designs. Honesty *(Lunaria annua)* produces shiny silver discs when the stems have been dried and the dark outer pods removed. Herb Robert, being a member of the cranesbill family, produces a seed-pod illustrating that name. Even the seedbox of the common poppy (*Papaver rhoeas*), though three-dimensional as a whole, can create a beautiful little 'wooden flower' if its fluted top is carefully sliced off.

MOSSES

Mosses are especially useful in miniature designs, where small, curving pieces can create the effect that a combination of curved stems and leaves might have made in a larger design. It is not until one begins collecting for the press that one realizes how many different shapes, sizes and shades of moss there are.

Drying:

TECHNIQUES IN DRYING

*J*ust as with preserving flowers and plants, drying plant material means that you always have something on hand with which to create a flower arrangement. There are two major methods of drying: drying flat and drying by hanging in bunches.

Drying Flat

This is the most commonly used method of drying flowers (either complete blooms or single petals), especially if they are to be used for other than decorative purposes. Petals should be detached carefully to avoid damaging or bruising them. Spread the petals and whole blooms out in a single layer on slatted shelves or between two sheets of newspaper in an airing cupboard, on newspaper and covered in muslin on trays in a warm, dry cupboard or near a central heating boiler. Prop the tray up on cotton reels to let the air circulate underneath if necessary. If you have an accessible attic, you could lay the flowers on muslin or net suspended, hammock-fashion, from the rafters. Drying may take from four to 10 days according to the flower and the humidity. They are ready when they feel crisp and rustle gently, like dry leaves, when lightly handled. To check whether they are completely dry, put one or two in a small air-tight jar and leave for a day or two. If condensation appears on the sides of the jar or on the bottom the flowers need to be dried a little more.

Flowers can also be dried in a plate-warming drawer or an ordinary oven, set to the lowest possible heat with the oven door propped open. This method will take only about an hour, but it requires more vigilance. Make sure the flowers do not become too warm – the temperature should be no higher than blood heat.

A microwave oven can also be used. Spread the petals or blooms out between sheets of absorbent paper and microwave for a minute, turning them over halfway through the drying process.

The small, electrically-powered home herb driers that are now available can also be used for drying flowers.

Hanging in Bunches

To dry flowers successfully by suspending them in bunches requires an atmosphere that is completely dry. There must be adequate ventilation and a good circulation of air, the temperature must be right and the flowers must be away from direct sunlight.

Not all flowers can be dried successfully. 'Everlasting' flowers change least when dried. Long-stemmed annual and perennial delphiniums, astilbe, lavender pink heathers, sea heathers, and leek and onion flower heads are some of the other most popular choices.

Group the flowers into bunches that are not too large so that the air can circulate, then tie the bunches fairly tightly, leaving a loop to hang them from. Suspend them, heads downwards, from separate hooks, a line or coathanger.

Methodology

Using a desiccant, such as powdered borax, sand, silica gel and proprietary mixtures, is the best way of preserving flowers that are to be used for ornamental purposes as it will remove the moisture from the flowers effectively and preserve the structure, shape and color of petals that would be spoilt by the other methods of drying.

Silica gel crystals, available from drugstores, are the most expensive desiccant. They can be crushed with a rolling pin to reduce the size of the crystals. Brand names for fine crystals are Lasting Flower and Flora-D Hydrate. Silica gel is the fastest-acting desiccant, producing dried blooms in only one to three days. The color of the flowers is therefore good but there is a tendency for them to become brittle if left in the desiccant for too long.

The silica gel mixture itself can be used over and over again, if after each application it is slowly dried out in a low-temperature oven. When you see blue crystals emerging, you know that the mixture has been reactivated.

Alum and borax can also be bought from the drugstore and these are inexpensive. They are particularly good for delicate petals. Allow seven to 10 days for the drying process. Borax often then needs a little encouragement to persuade it to come away from the dried flowers.

ABOVE *1 To wire flower heads before drying, remove most of the stem and push stub wire through the flower center. Coil the extra wire around the base of the flower for support.*

ABOVE *2 Cover the bottom of a deep, airtight container with the desiccant. Lay the flowers on it according to their shape and size – smaller flowers face down, larger ones on their sides.*

The blooms can be given false stems after drying by carefully inserting florists' wire or even pipe cleaners (although these are not as good). Flower heads are easier to wire before drying. Cut off most of the stem then push a piece of wire down through the center of the flower, or, if easier, depending on the bloom, push the wire up through the stem end. Coil the wire round neatly below the flower to support it.

Cover the base of a large, deep tin, such as a baking sheet, with about ½–1 in (1.5–2.5 cm) of desiccant, carefully smoothing out any lumps. Lay petals or flowers without stems on the desiccant in accordance with their shape – for example, pansies and buttercups should be placed face down while fragile flowers like hollyhocks should be laid on their sides. If the flowers have stems place a wire mesh over or in the tin and insert the flowers, heads uppermost. Gently sift the desiccant around the flowers then carefully let it fall naturally in between the petals and right into the centre of each bloom, using a fine brush or skewer if necessary to ease it into place, until the blooms are completely covered. Trumpet-shaped flowers are an exception, they should be filled with desiccant before being covered. Cover the tin with an airtight lid then leave it somewhere warm, dark and dry.

The texture and thickness of the petals and the density of the blooms will govern the length of time they will take to dry. Lawn daisies, for example, should be ready in two days whereas African marigolds need two weeks.

Carefully pour off the desiccant, allowing the petals and flowers to drop into your hand. If the flowers feel papery with no signs of dampness they are sufficiently dry. If they do not, dry them for a little longer.

Brush away any remaining desiccant with the point of a fine brush. Any petals that have come away from complete heads can be stuck back in place using a transparent glue and a wooden cocktail stick. Add a few crystals of silica gel to the container if the flowers or petals are to be stored just in case there is any rogue moisture.

LEFT *3 Gently sift or pour the desiccant over the flowers, allowing it to fall between the petals and into the flower center. Continue until the flowers are completely covered.*

RIGHT *6 When drying intricate or delicate flowers, it may be necessary to brush away any remaining desiccant between the petals with the point of a fine brush.*

ABOVE *4 Close the container with an airtight lid and leave in a warm, dry place. When the crystals turn from blue to white, the flower moisture has been absorbed.*

ABOVE *5 Carefully pour off the desiccant. If the flowers are ready, they will feel papery and completely dry. If not, replace them in the crystals for a little longer.*

DRIED FLOWER ARRANGEMENTS

*I*n the winter months, when there are few fresh flowers to work with, dried flowers can provide particularly welcome decoration for the home. Large designs can fill empty fireplaces or the unused corners of rooms, and smaller arrangements can be made as center-pieces for occasional tables or mantlepieces. It is well worth putting time and trouble into your designs, since they will continue to look appealing for many months after you complete them.

With dried material, you can be very inventive in choosing containers since there is no problem of water seepage to consider. Pieces of driftwood, weathered wood and bark found on rambles might be employed, perhaps, or, for something more unusual, you could buy lengths of metal piping.

Dried flowers can also be used to decorate small boxes or wastepaper baskets, and they can make delightful pictures to hang on the wall. Miniatures can be really charming, but here it is important to choose material in the right proportion and you will need tweezers to set the material in place. This may seem slow exercise but it can be very satisfying to complete such a picture. Old frames, which can be cleaned and resprayed, are often to be found in salerooms.

A clear glass dome placed over an arrangement of dried flowers looks very effective and provides the additional benefit of protecting the flowers from dust. Make the found-ation for the arrangement out of foam or fine wire mesh formed to a suitable shape then insert flowers to build up an attractive display.

Useful Flowers for Dried Arrangements

There is always a vast and exciting choice of dried materials available from the florists, but if you grow your own flowers many of them can be dried very easily at home.

Some subjects dry more attractively than others. For example, if delphiniums are cut just before maturity, they will eventually dry out keeping an almost perfect color. They are best cut when about half the spikes show full color. They should then be stood in about 2in (5cm) of water and allowed to condition thoroughly. Then hang them upside-down in a dry, draught-free place until they gradually dry out. A light coating with clear spray will help to keep the florets in place.

ACHILLEA retains its golden color for several years.

HELICHRYSUMS AND STATICE are very popular as dried materials. They supply a wonderful variety of both color and form. For people who grow their own helichrysums, remember to insert a wire through the flower head as soon as it is cut as, once it dries, it becomes almost too hard to pierce. Try to insert the wire up through a short stem so that it does not show. Then hang the flowers upside-down in bunches ready for using in your winter arrangements.

HYDRANGEAS also keep their color, particularly the green and red varieties, but the pale blue variety turns brown, although it is useful for masking the foam. It is best to strip the foliage from hydrangeas before leaving them to dry out.

MOLUCELLA bleaches to a delicate cream tint as it gradually dries. Arranged with grasses or fabric flower, it makes very elegant line material and is long lasting.

ROSES, also, can be dried on their natural stems, while almost any flower head can be quickly and successfully dried in silica gel. You need quite a large quantity, for the heads should be arranged in layers and copiously covered with the gel. This is available from most good drugstores or from specialist suppliers of flower arranging materials.

LEFT This is a 'petite' arrangement, which is defined as one under 9in (23cm) in size. The shell container was picked up on the beach and glued to another shell for use as a base.

Materials: *shell container, soaked floral foam. Dried flowers of dyed sea lavender, xeranthemum, statice, tansy, santolina; hare's-tail grass.*

1 Insert the sea lavender to give a curving outline. 2 Add the xeranthemums to the outside and over the rim. 3 Add the statice, tansy and santolina to the centre. 4 Fill in with a few hare's-tails and a little more sea lavender.

LEFT Design in sepia.

Materials: *marble container, two photos with frames, brown base, cream lace drape, stick in bottle, modelling clay, soaked floral foam in candle-cup placed on top of marble container.*

Glycerined plant material including dock, foxglove, seedheads, beech, laurel, yew, eucalyptus, Grevillea robusta; dried flowers of statice, helichrysum, gypsophila (baby's breath); a few skeletonized magnolia leaves; hare's-tail and pampas grasses.

1 Insert dock, hare's-tail and pampas to give a triangular outline. 2 Add foxglove seedheads, statice and helichrysum. 3 Add a few more hare's-tails lower down. 4 Place skeletonized magnolia beech and laurel near the middle, along with a few more flowers. 5 Fill in the gaps with small pieces of eucalyptus, grevillea and gypsophila. 6 Arrange laurel leaves so that they flow over the rim with the magnolias and pampas. 7 Place on the base, which has been positioned on the cream lace drape. The material is held up at the back by a stick secured in a bottle with modelling clay. Add the photographs to complete the design.

BELOW LEFT This is a design interpreting wood-carving. The wood-like structure of the various pods helps to further the theme, and the different shades of brown are the varying colours of woods.

Materials: *tin can with dry floral foam, wood slice. Dried and preserved material, including poinciana pods, coconut spathes, proteas, tulip seedheads, eucalyptus, cones, beech leaves.*

1 Insert a large poinciana pod and coconut spathe at the back. 2 Add proteas and tulip pods, and bring other material to form a slightly curving outline. 3 Fill in with the heavy plant material at the centre, and a few preserved leaves to fill in the gaps. 4 Place to one side on the wooden slab.

Index